To Photograph a Snow Crystal

Paul Batchelor

Smith/Doorstop Books

Published 2006 by
Smith/Doorstop Books
The Poetry Business
The Studio
Byram Arcade
Westgate
Huddersfield HD1 1ND

Copyright © Paul Batchelor 2006
All Rights Reserved

ISBN 1-902382-82-X
Typeset at The Poetry Business
Printed by Swiftprint, Huddersfield

The Poetry Business gratefully acknowledges the help of Arts Council England and Kirklees Metropolitan Council.

Acknowledgements

Many thanks to the editors of the following, in which some of these poems first appeared: *Modern Poetry in Translation*, *Poetry Review*, *Poetry Wales*, *Shearsman, Stride, Tower Poetry.*

Thanks also to the Society of Authors and *New Writing North*

CONTENTS

5	To Photograph a Kingfisher
7	Afterwards
9	Snow
11	The Permafrost: an A – Z
13	Lebiyska Mova
15	Tristia
20	Keening
21	Findings
24	Snow Melt
26	To Photograph a Snow Crystal
27	*Notes on the poems*

TO PHOTOGRAPH A KINGFISHER

    A bracket exposure.
At Limerick market
    your grandfather's grandfather
is selling a kingfisher.
    A gypsy in love
with long distances, he
    is travelling light:
a basket of eggs,
    the names of his women.
A song for each one
    is easily carried.

    Previsualise.
Turning out a bag
    of scraps & clippings,
feeling the baby
    kick inside her,
your grandfather's mother
    is making a hooky mat
in the likeness of a kingfisher.
    A parallax:
her husband is planning
    to take up with a fancy woman.

    Widen the aperture.
Your grandfather is finding
    the body of a kingfisher
in a glim of ice.
    He cradles the crush
of orange & blue
    as he'll nurse his daughter
through rheumatic fever,
    carrying her out
like a basket of eggs
    when the doctor won't come.

    Develop, agitate.
Like a rumour of winter
    in living colour
there is the kingfisher
    caught in the frame,
a snapshot memento
    like a lock of red hair
easily carried
    easily held
between finger & thumb
    as if for safe-keeping.

AFTERWARDS

I saw you lug
a laundry bag

down an unfamiliar street,
stuff sheets & knickers into a machine, discrete,

& while you thumbed a 6-months-old magazine,
knelt to watch them spin.

I saw you smack a kiss
of air & lipgloss,

cruelly
dab your wrists with essence of patchouli,

dash blusher across
each cheek yet somehow miss

me in the mirror
wide-eyed for the ceremony of mascara.

I was even there when you prepared that meal:
I saw you give the basil leaves

a brisk rinse & scoop
the extra cup

of rice
into the pan. If I had a voice

I'd be all advice,
but truth to tell I hardly recognise

you, what with your hair
cut in a bob, what with that red dress you wear

for him… This new life took me by surprise.
I'd prise

the lid off that jar & spear an olive
on a toothpick for you, if I were alive.

SNOW

You find yourself inside a nest of papers,
reading the odd line, tearing off a strip
of shopping list & Valentine; reminder & thankyou;
pornographic doodles she made on your receipts
when she waitressed at *The Copper Kettle*…
You've already destroyed your life's work, or,
if not destroyed, turned into origami boats
you didn't know you had it in you to make.
At 4 a.m. you start on the letters
from your first summer spent apart
(exact descriptions of what she planned to do
& what she wanted you to do when you met)
then stuff you kept for the sheer hell of it:
two scratched CDs (Kate Bush, Al Green),
a clutch of reconciliation notes,
artless descriptions of how she suffered
with a broken heart & period pains,
& all the postcards (Miro, Shiele, Chagall,
Kandinsky and Bonnard): you shred the lot.
At 6 a.m. you steady yourself to make a cup of tea.
Familiar shapes emerge: the tipsy profile of a bookcase,
the guitar on its stand, practising yoga,
a shot-glass, a broken shoe, the spines of books
someone scattered in their hurry, a pizza-box
of crusts, used condoms wrapped in toilet roll
(needless to say, you don't recall
with whom you spent the night),
a loop of hair on the pillow, the smell of stale

debauchery… You raise the shade.
Cathedral bells have put on airs.
The streets are innocent with snow.
Everywhere the beautiful
unwanted daughters of the very poor
totter to work on mock-fashionable shoes
past news-stands that demand a referendum
& flaunt exclusives on Victoria Beckham's
damage-limitation dress.
Shutters roll & market traders lug
crates & set out stalls.
A drunk curled in a doorway sleeps it off
while five pound notes fall, melting on his tongue.
The city rubs its eyes. The Metro starts
its running commentary. Your hangover asserts itself
& junkmail shudders through the letterbox.

Here, where another poet might begin,
is where you end: a blank page of Suprematist perfection,
the invisible republic
of Kazimir Malevich, no justified line
to take, no rule of thumb to break, no margin
in which to hide. A day
with nothing to say for itself, and morning
making light of it. Who in the world
might she have been? You draw the blinds
& turn back to the bed as one
by one the panes fill up with snow.

THE PERMAFROST: AN A – Z

The Permafrost is quietly spoken, disliking sudden noise or sudden gesture. Despite this, it is remarkably hospitable, enjoying long hours of easy talk, during which one might detect its eagerness to agree.

The Permafrost is able to convince, but rarely to persuade. The uninitiated see nothing but scrubland, and complain of 'being cold.' By such signs are they to be identified.

The Permafrost must never be referred to as *tundra*.

The Permafrost sounds like an ailing synthesiser. It is 1982 at the best of times. "They used to grow grapes here," the natives boast. How little must have been promised these people; how little they must feel they are owed: they do not even refer to their ancestors as 'we.'

The Permafrost is noted for an absence of birdsong: a policy of the leisure & tourism industry.

The Permafrost is surrounded by hills & small mountains. Many resemble the sleeping forms of females. A policy of the leisure & tourism industry.

The Permafrost is densely populated, despite its reputation. Colonies are rare, but not unknown. Usually, an individual will acquire a smallholding with the intention of using it as a holiday home or retreat. All will tell you they are passing through. More & more residents are choosing to raise families there.

The Permafrost can draw surprising admissions from some residents, who liken it to the process of hypnosis. You are encouraged to keep a record of your stay.

The Permafrost is a voluntary organisation, run by dedicated individuals who have taken time out of their busy schedules. It accepts no responsibility for belongings including articles of clothing that are lost or damaged during your stay. It does not supply consumables.

The Permafrost handles unpredictably in confined spaces & is capable of elaborate structures when base restrictions are applied. It can be likened to a panic room & the anxiety induced by knowing such a place exists.

The Permafrost is habitually frugal, but will occasionally disarm with a show of generosity, as in the provision of blotting paper or funeral meats. Nothing is grudged because nothing is given: complimentary gifts are covered by your initial payment.

The Permafrost is carpeted throughout with a fully up-to-date kitchen & self-cleaning oven. Relax in a peaceful environment free from distractions. A curfew is currently in operation, exact times to be announced.

LEBIYSKA MOVA

He tells of Kobzari
       making their rounds
    at fairs & markets –
       blind street-singers
       keepers of a secret history
           the struggle
               for the Black Sea steppe
           Cossack rebellions
              fallen heroes
           the cruelty of the Turk –

Of impeccably played bandura
        & Fedir the Cold One
          sleeping in a ditch –
    Fedir with a voice
        like a jet of blood with grief in it
       proclaiming the truth
           in *lebiyska mova*
           a gospel in tomorrow's language –

Of a village where the butcher starves
   the shoemaker goes barefoot
  & someone saws a bed in half
      to make a bed

Died, all, in the terror

In a Mission
in Colonia Esperanca
    he composes
  a final *dumy*
    explaining
        to the anthropologist
        with his reel-to-reel
    that when the pitch is bent
   & sharp or flat notes
     slip into the scale
    it is called
      dodavaty zhaloshchiv:
     'adding the sorrow'

TRISTIA

*

My friend, until you have been cursed
to wander, kinless, foreign lands where range
barbarians so foul the farmer goes
with a machete strung across his back
simply to milk his kine, you cannot know
time's secret ministries: how it can crawl
like a disease that steals
so sly upon a man he barely feels
its subtle victories; or like an army
marching at half speed. It's true: I have bogged-down
in this forgotten outpost. Do not upbraid
narrowness of theme: I never wrote
to better purpose than when I implore
Augustus to be merciful.

*

I have bogged-down in this forgotten outpost
on the Black Sea: a spit of land, a fistula
in the oxter of an Empire I once served.
In winter, the ocean freezes. Brigands
drive chariots over the ice, terrorize
farmers, raze the homesteads. Women
& livestock are seized while men are lashed
to stakes, compelled to watch their crops destroyed.
Leander might have found apt use
for such a frozen waste: he would have walked
the Hellespont like a vault of glass, but those old
tales are not told here. Winter is cruel.
I think continually of my last night in Rome.
Wolves move nimbly on the ice to bring down deer.

*

I watch you wave, & when you disappear
become a house where nobody lives;
an old façade decayed; a pillow bereft
of the smell of your hair. A stranger asks
but nobody can mind who lived in that
boarded-up ruin children say is haunted,
where manuscripts lie strewn about the floor;
where lemon trees have over-run the orchard;
where, in the quartered fields, stogged wheat
reeks like a byre & rape holds sway.
You wave your arms & crows
scatter like crows. And that's the pose
in which I've held you – waiting, open armed –
for seven years. And I'm still here.

*

The gods flee to the stars, where they become
daft stories poets use
to show their mastery of form;
an exercise in rhyme.

Perhaps a corner yet remains in Rome
that holds in reverence the name
of one who versed with bite:
wherever poets meet

let the best chair stand empty:
let them remember
Naso, who would not stoop to wring
old metre from a heathen tongue;

who shamed the gods with his inventions –
& found men less forgiving.

*

Quarantine or quest,
in exile blessed or cursed,
the ocean will be crossed
after our man has lost
everything to a thirst
beyond fathom: at the last
he will kneel before the polestar,
salute the god of this great vast.

Does he recall the aftertaste
of those tears he kissed
away? Or her blush the first
time he saw her undressed?
Who is it waits for Naso, palms pressed
together, as the ocean waits to be crossed?

KEENING

The quality of keening is not narrow.
It ranges freely, back roads & low roads:
a violin heard from a window at night
(a silken rubbing, a tune you can't place),
a fellside lapwing signalling in slate grey rain:
all this betokens keening. It travels incognito
as lyric, or as perfume from a dress,
passes customs unfazed; is taken as currency
everywhere, ache bearing witness to ache.
Keening puts words in hungry mouths,
gives tongue without language, longing without hope.
With keening no man's hand is strong,
no heart true. It mars the wild
& we who were not wild enough are marred
equally. Truly your riches are worthless;
your poverty yet shall be rendered more bitter
with keening, who has no tears. Let blood be drawn
& let the dogs be driven far from the hearth
before keening shares tears: beholden to no one,
it suffers all woes, that none may evade it.

FINDINGS

1

He settles in the burn
till snow-melt smooths his young face younger still.
I would recall
all the lost places of his life & find them new again,
the images to which he will return:
a fossil of two fern leaves, which he found & gave to me;
a nest
of baby weasels, bald & reptilian.

He says *We'd best work fast*,
& drops his handkerchief into the nest:
the cauldron seethes: claws & teeth
needle the handkerchief.
When they're attached, he lifts a clutch
of weasels up for me to see.

2

My body will blacken and turn into coal.
                    A Johnny Cash *basso profundo*
echoes around the house-end: Dark as a Dungeon,
                                        Chicken Road.
Jimmie Rodgers, Tennessee Ernie Ford.
Trouble In Mind, Come Back to Sorrento.
An old song travels lightly. What about a garage full
of dead TV sets, vacuum cleaners, knick-knacks
that never quite took off? A cartridge player & a Betamax
video he stayed faithful to.

What about a shadow on the lung? A blockage. An obstruction
found by chance. A routine check-up. Tests. Endoscopies,
appointments, cancellations, new appointments, consultations…
The doctors' names grow nearly reassuring.
A papery handshake from a specialist.
An x-ray of two fern leaves on the screen.

3

In '36
I worked at Kielder forest, snedding trees.
There was this burn where I would go to wash at lowse,
just like a fox –
I laughed: a fox?
But when I pictured you, pearls snaking from your mouth & nose,
I saw, behind the river's mirror, waiting for the hunt to lose
his trail, a fox –

till you corrected me: when a fox is full of lice
he settles in a burn, his snout above the water,
a twig between his teeth. I have no
idea if this is true. The lice
swarm over him & gather
on the twig. When it is full, he lets it go: so.

SNOW MELT

winter pasture,
clotted rain –
snow first-footing
the new year

*

bridled with ice
the beck is down:
it has been snowing
it will snow

*

threading moor
& skyline together,
a red threat of fox
flagging the field

stand silently & go

*

a world spins
wintering
under each
eye-lid

*

knuckled feet
gather in –

blade of the spine
an upturned boat

*

this is a man:
body of Christ
life in his teeth
snow in his mouth

stand silently & go

*

melt & make
no noise – this life,
this crucible
of accidents

*

is ice what happens
when water forgets
how to be anything
else?

*

snow-melt over-
fills the burn –
stots off stone,
tells it clean

stand silently & go

TO PHOTOGRAPH A SNOW CRYSTAL

       Hokkaido, '54.
Ukichiro Nakaya
       coaxes a crystal
into life on a rabbit hair
       in an unlikely menagerie
of stellar dendrites
       double stars
sectored plates
       crystal twins
clusters, bullets
       & chandeliers.
The fickle, six-fold
       symmetry of snowflakes.
The fourteen identified
       varieties of ice.
Why do complex patterns
       arise spontaneously
in simple physical
       systems? Trust me, love,
to make heavy weather
       of first principles.
What might I make
       of these arabesques;
facets & lattices,
       glyphs & ciphers,
the shapes with which
       you decorate your poems?

Notes on the poems

'The Permafrost: an A-Z'
Written while under the influence of the Magazine
album *Secondhand Daylight* (1979).

'Lebiyska Mova'
'Lebiyska Mova' is a secret language spoken by
the Kobzari: itinerant musicians of Ukraine. The
Kobzari sang epic cycles of songs known as 'dumy,'
telling of Ukrainian history and the wars that
formed the country. A bandura is a lap harp with
fifty five strings. The Kobzari had guilds, designated
territories, and an oral tradition thousands of years
old. In other respects (such as their ambivalent
social status as beggars/entertainers, and the fact
that they were often blind) they were comparable
to bluesmen such as Charlie Patton or Blind Willie
McTell. The greatest Kobzari, Fedir, travelled where
he liked. A misanthrope, Fedir slept in ditches
between gigs and was nicknamed 'the Cold One.'
In 1933, Stalin declared the Kobzari 'enemies of the
people,' and within a few years all but a handful
disappeared.

'Tristia'
In AD 8, Augustus Caesar relegated Publius
Ovidius Naso to Tomis (now Constanza in
Romania), officially because of the licentiousness
of Ovid's *Ars Amatoria*. As this was published ten
years earlier, it is unlikely to be the genuine reason.
'Relegation' (rather than 'exile') meant that Ovid
retained his citizenship. This legal technicality had

two major consequences: Ovid's wife would remain in Rome to look after his affairs, and a pardon from Augustus remained a possibility. So Ovid spent his time in Tomis writing *Tristia*: love poems to his wife, and poems of petition (aimed indirectly at Augustus) to be circulated around the capital. These are loose versions of various poems from *Tristia* and *Epistulae Ex Ponto*.

'Keening'
i.m. Barry MacSweeney

'Findings'
i.m. William Oswald Young

'Snow Melt'
Written in response to a series of photographs by Sylvia Sukop.

'To Photograph a Snow Crystal'
for Anna Woodford
Ukichiro Nakaya was the first person to grow a snow crystal synthetically in a laboratory. At sub-zero temperatures, most materials frost over, covering the individual snow crystals. Nakaya found that the natural oils in rabbit hair prevented the nucleation of ice: he could therefore suspend a snow crystal on a hair, and watch it develop.